Thank you for choosing our small publishing company. We greatly appreciate your support, which allows us to continue bringing unique and inspiring books to people like you. If you enjoyed this book, please consider leaving a review. Your feedback not only helps fellow crafters discover exceptional graphics but also supports independent publishers like us in our mission to share unique books with the world. We value your input and look forward to hearing your thoughts.

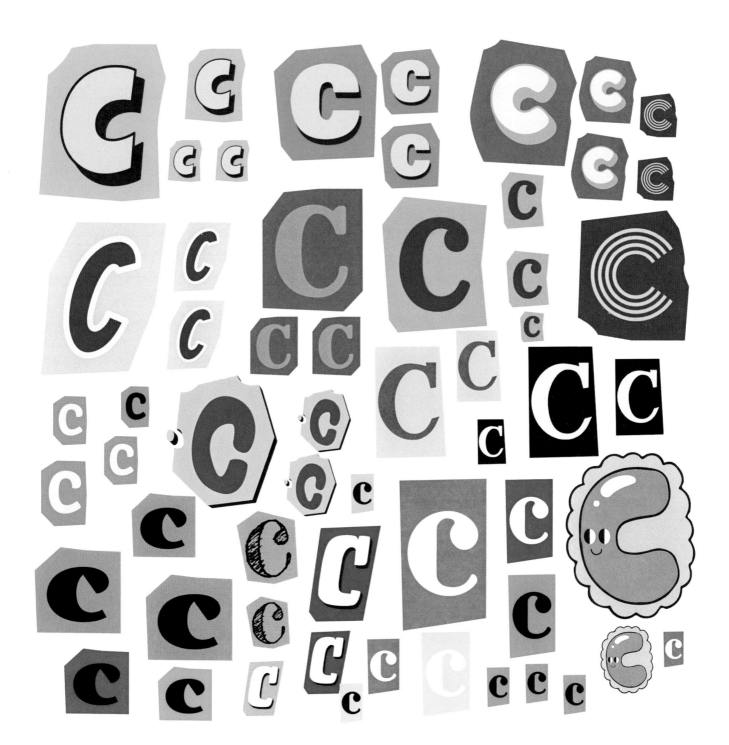

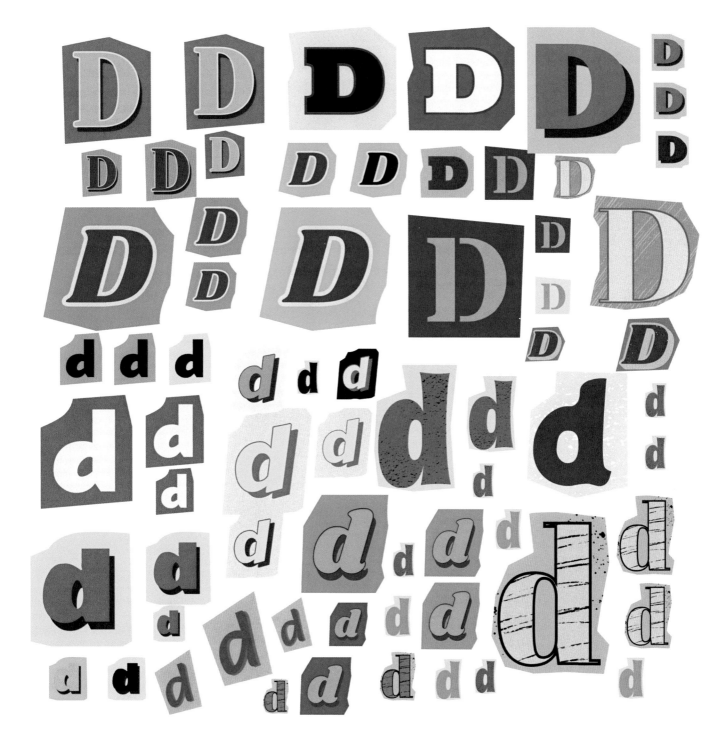

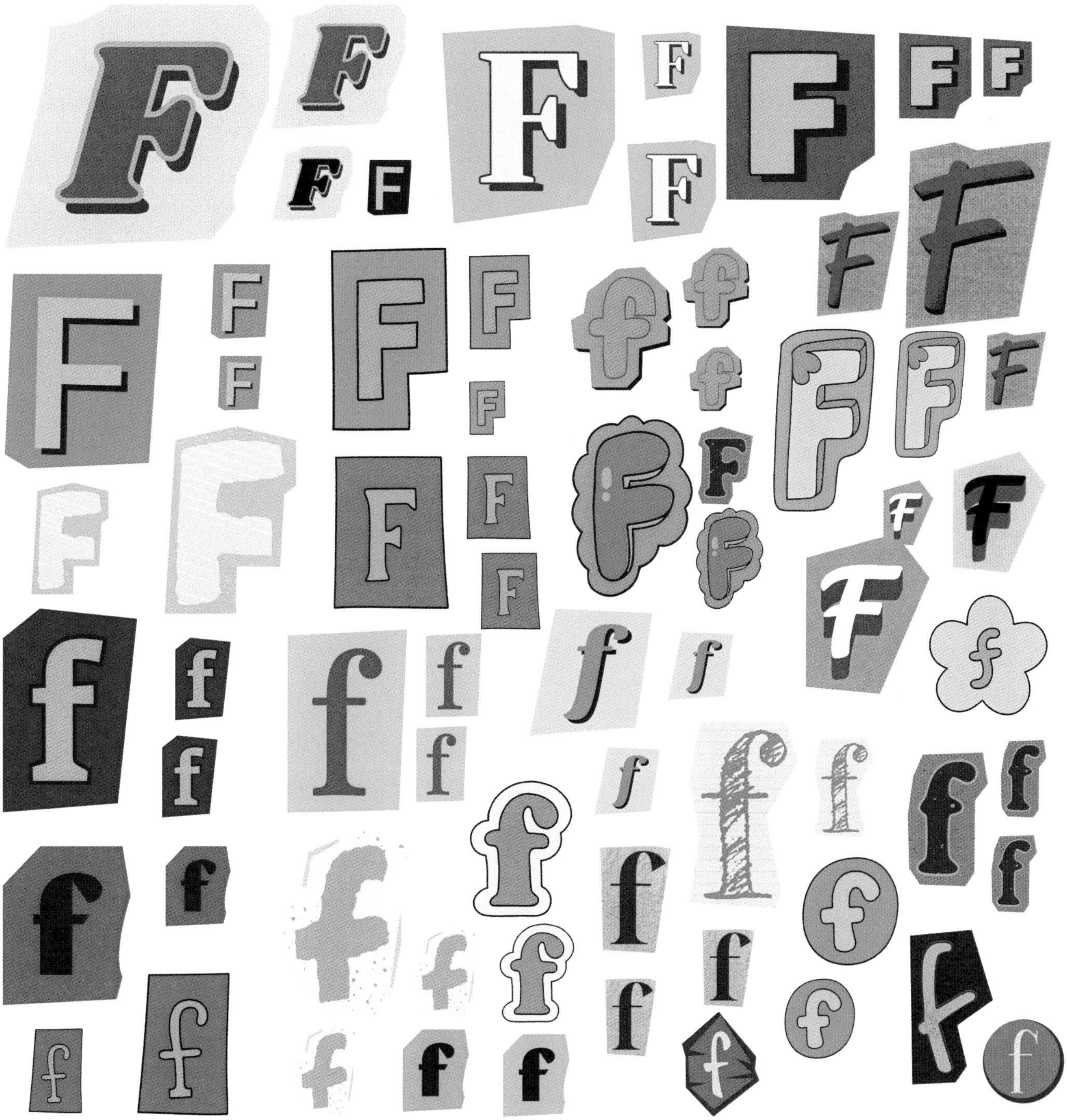

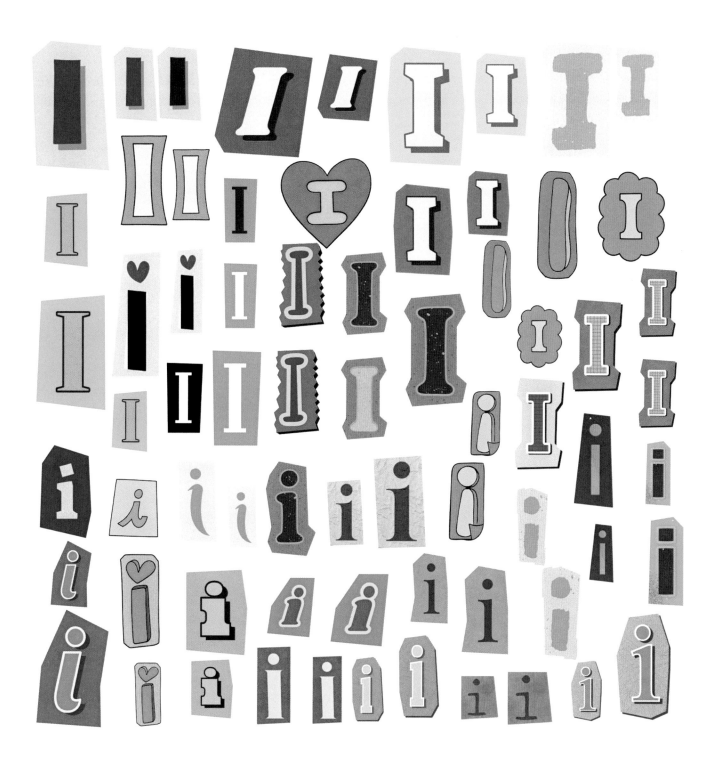

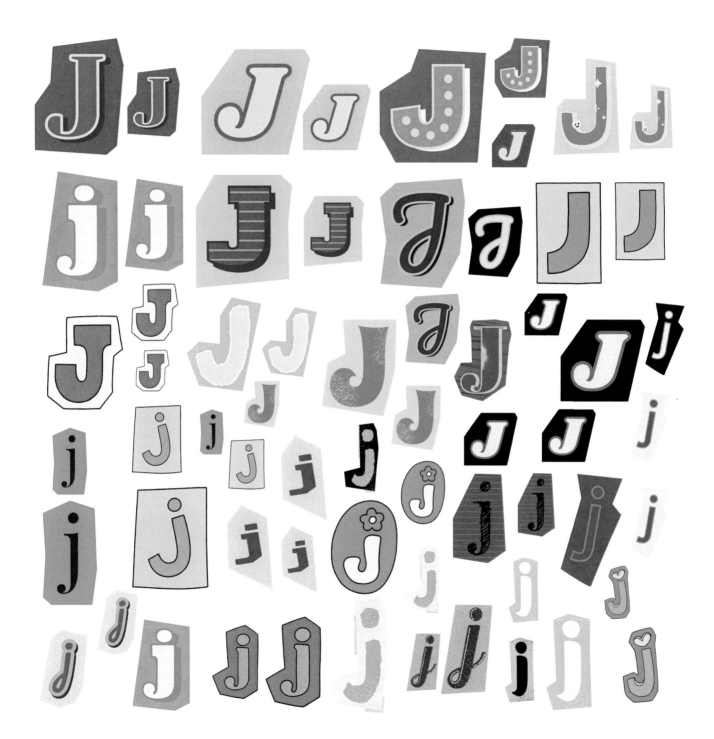

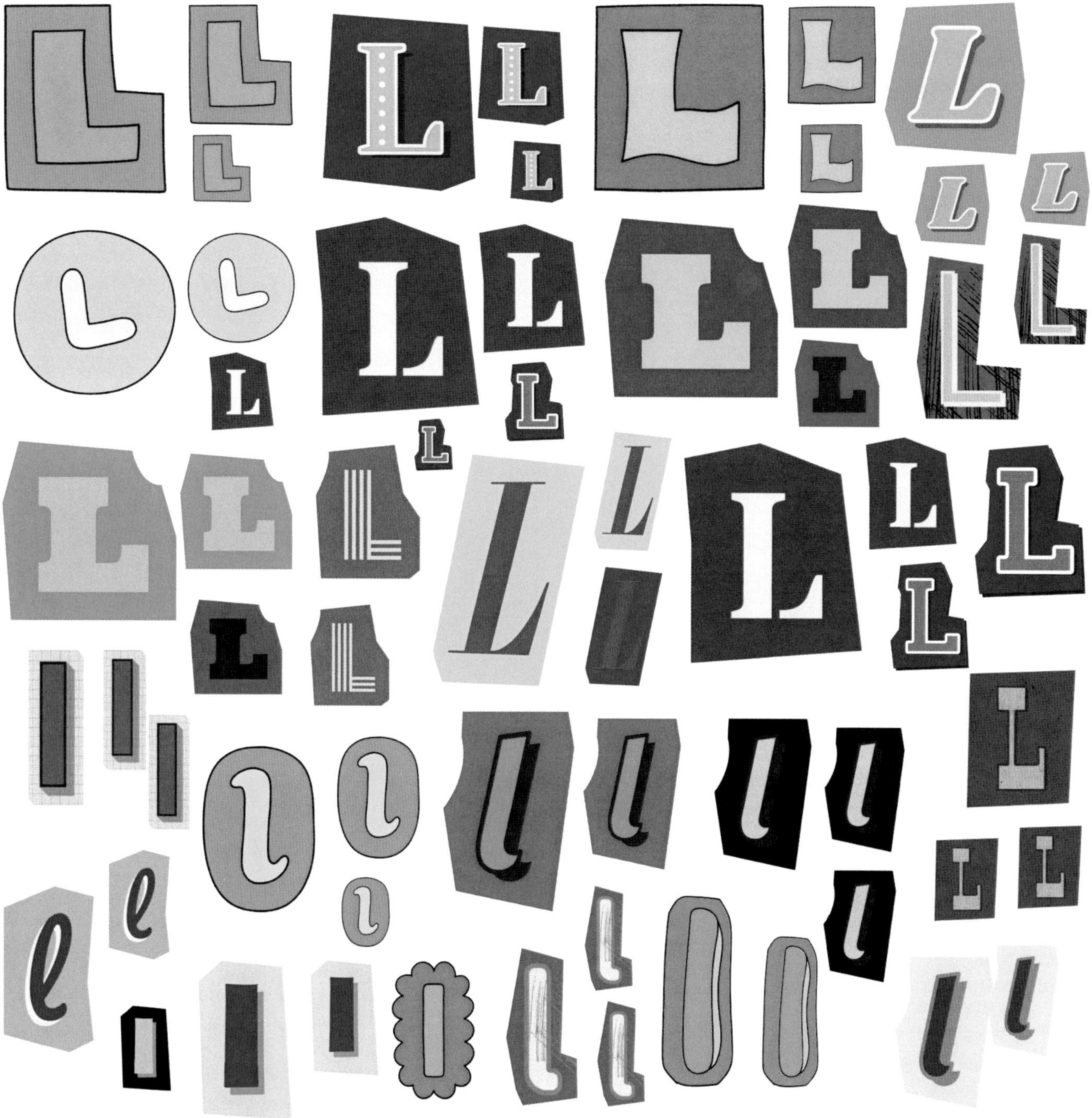

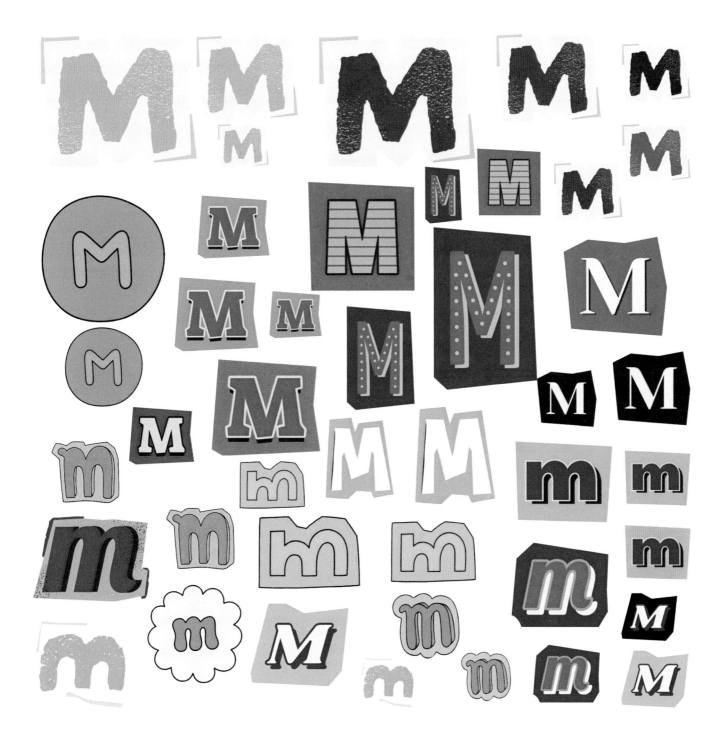

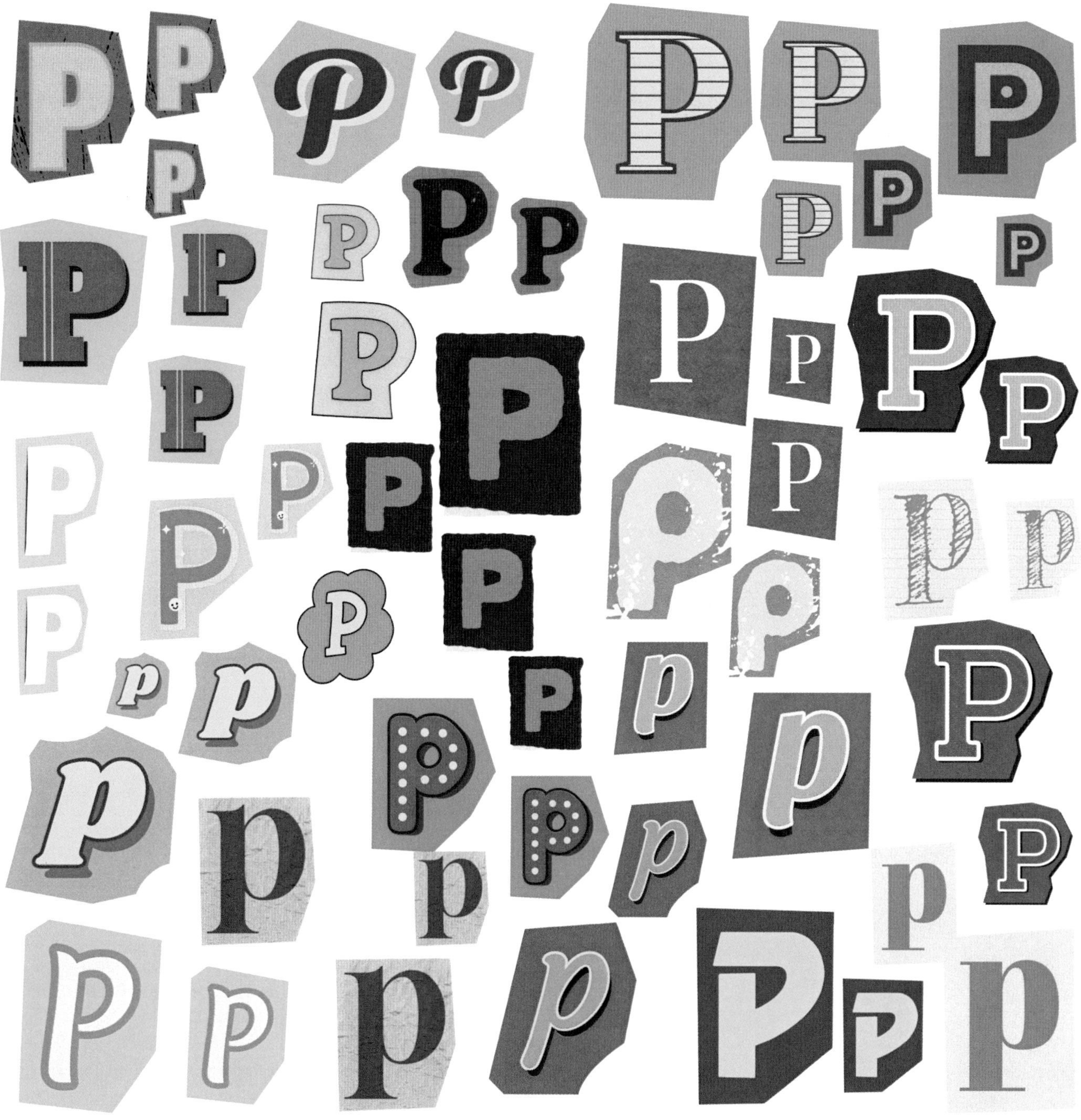

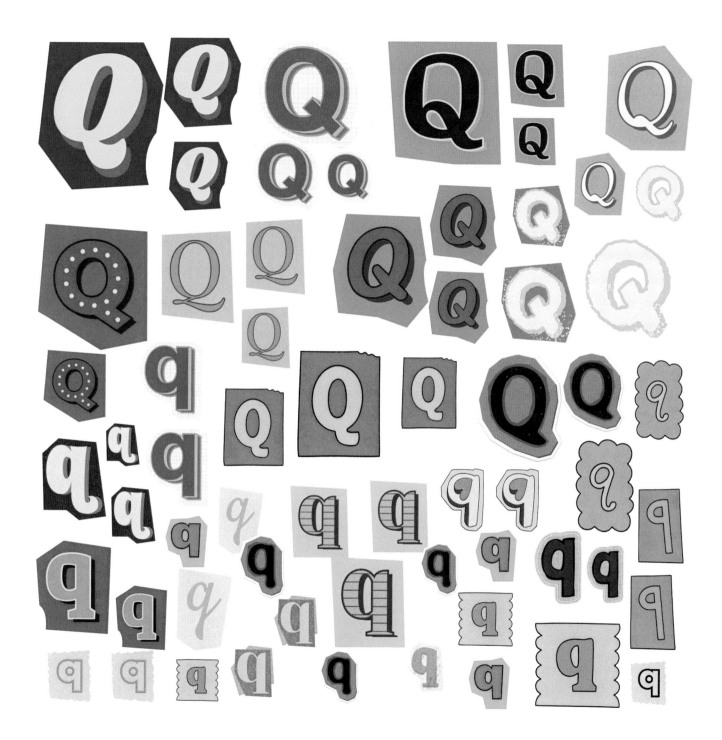

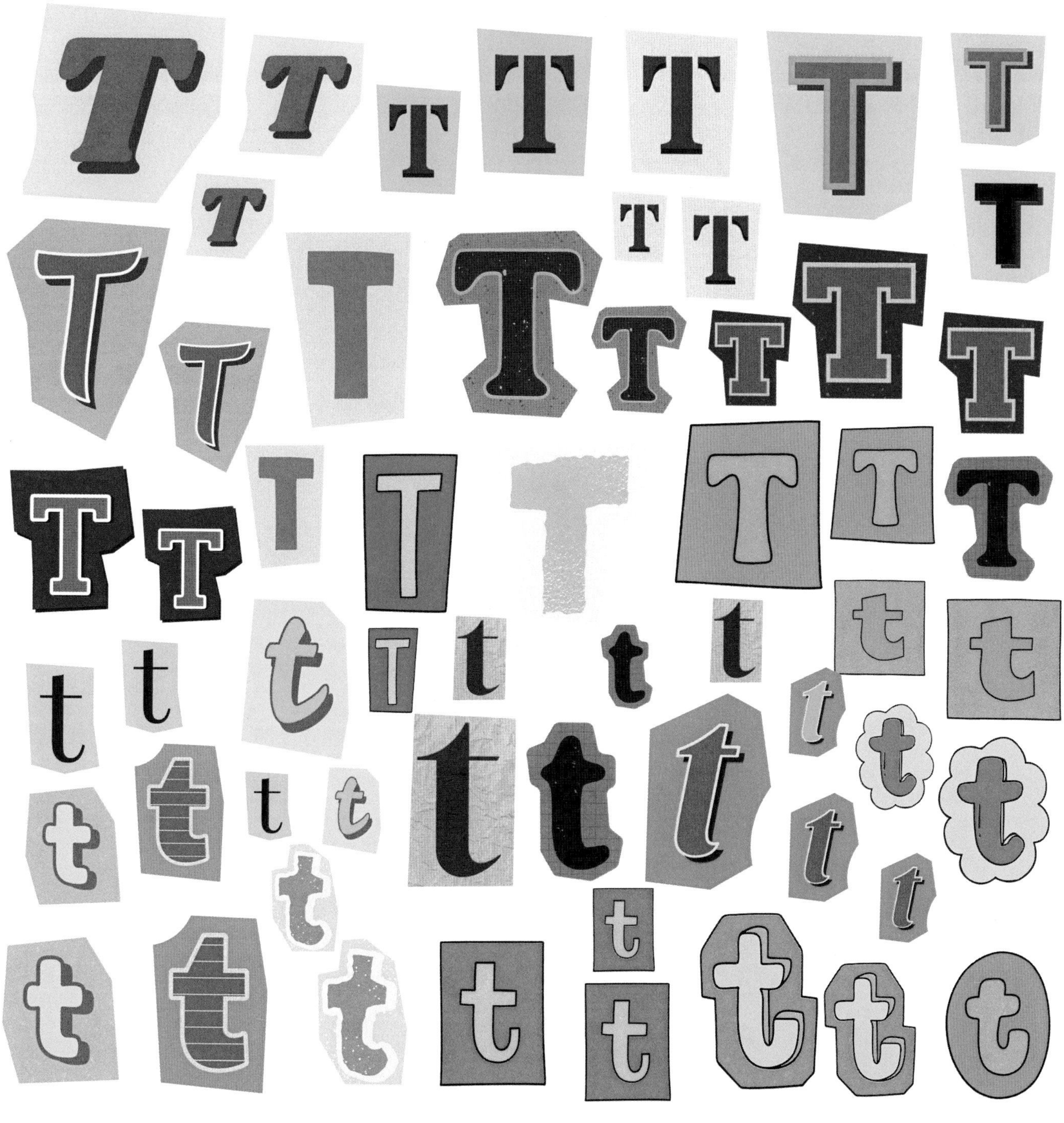

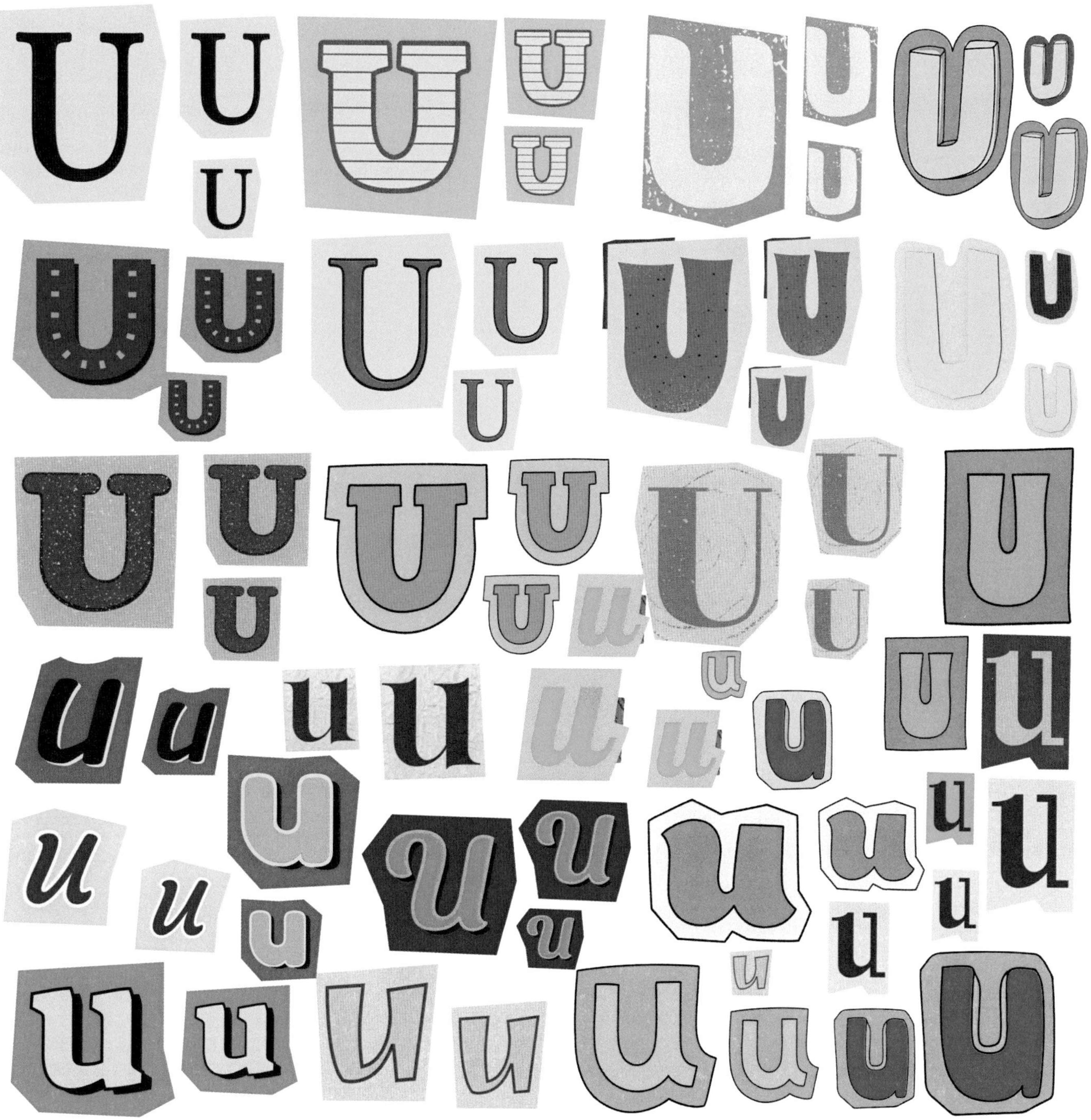

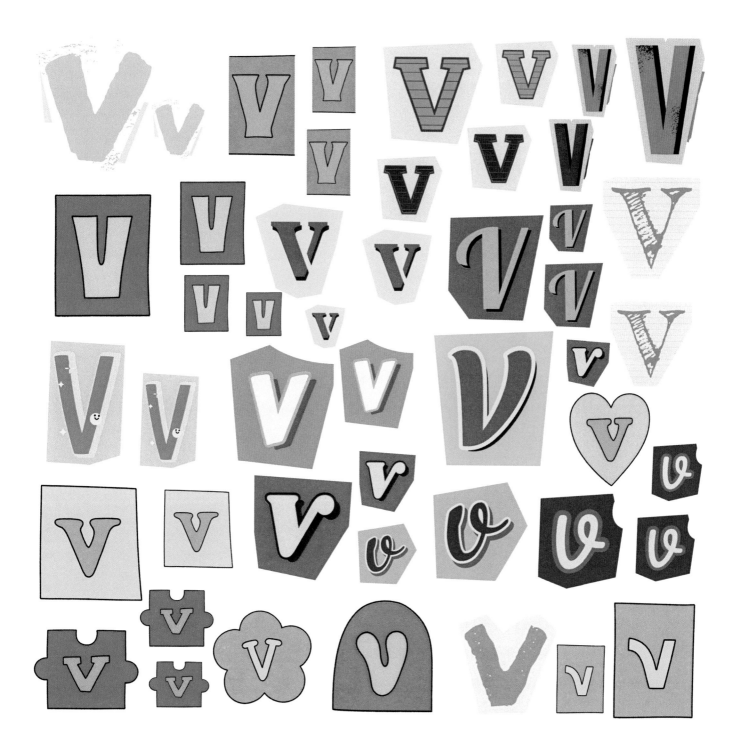

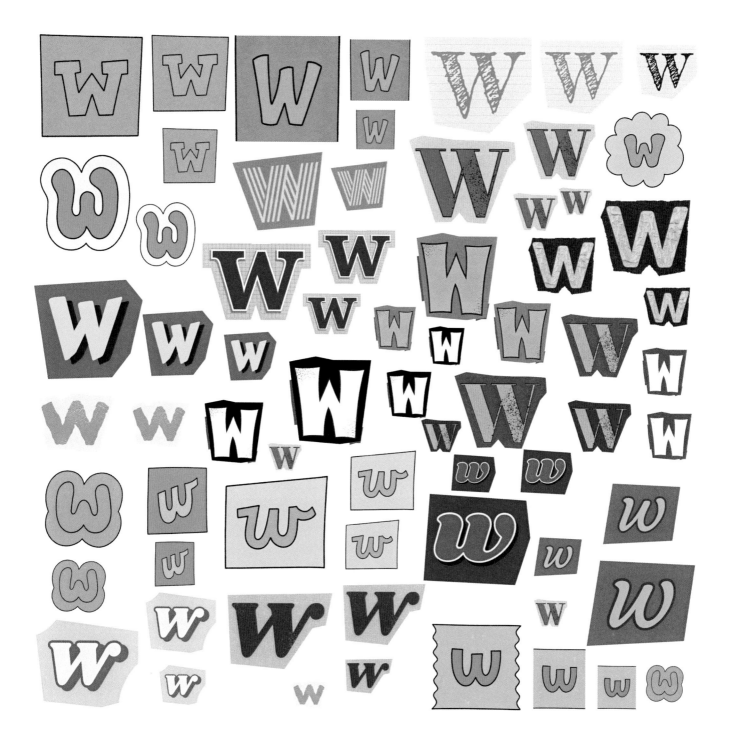

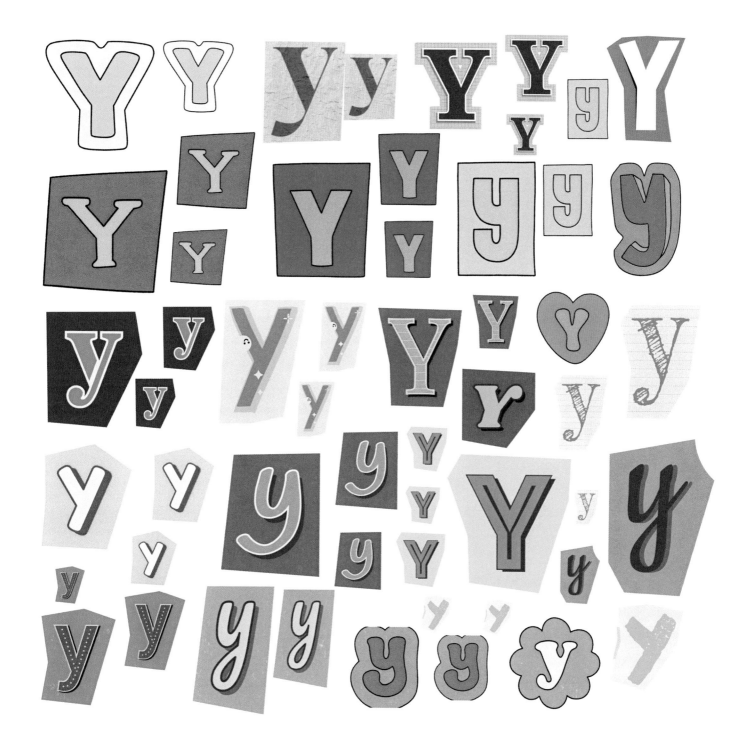

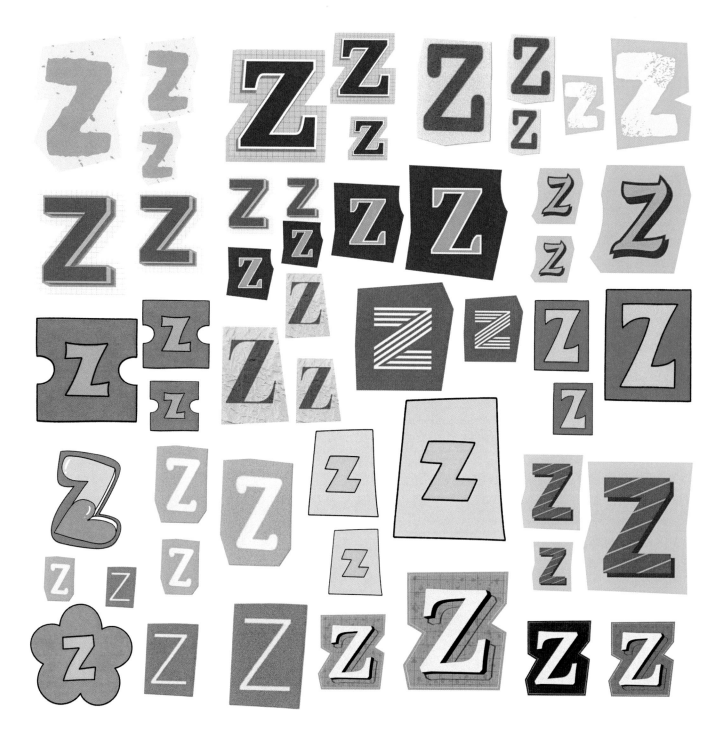

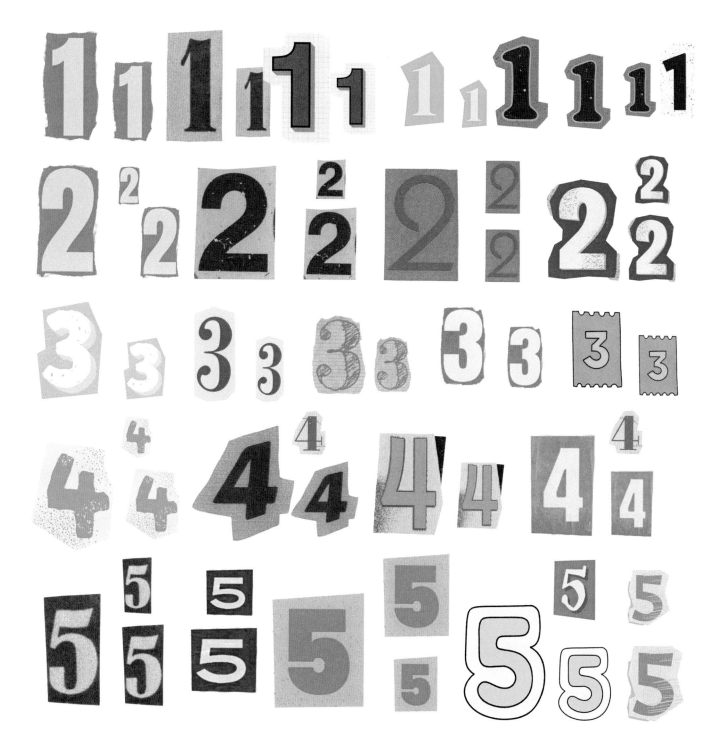

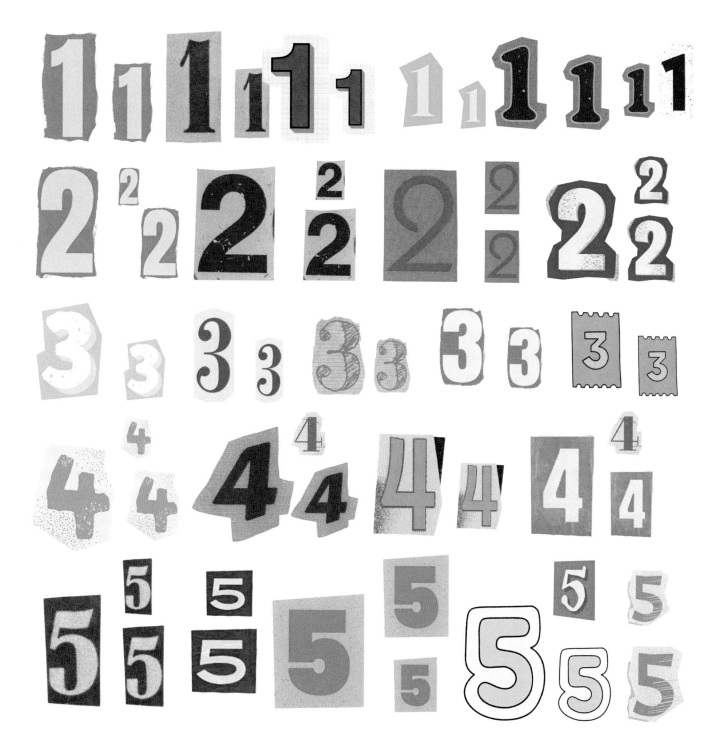

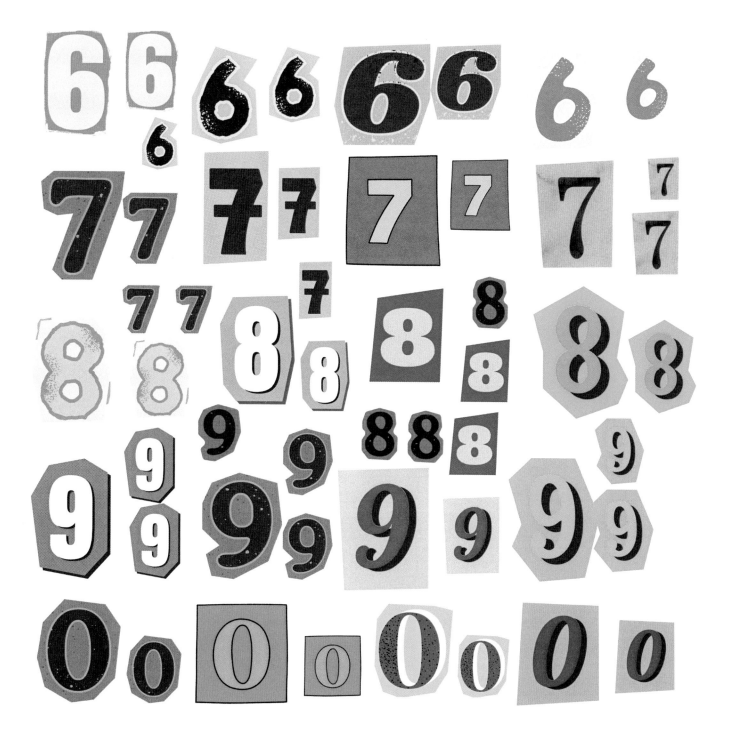

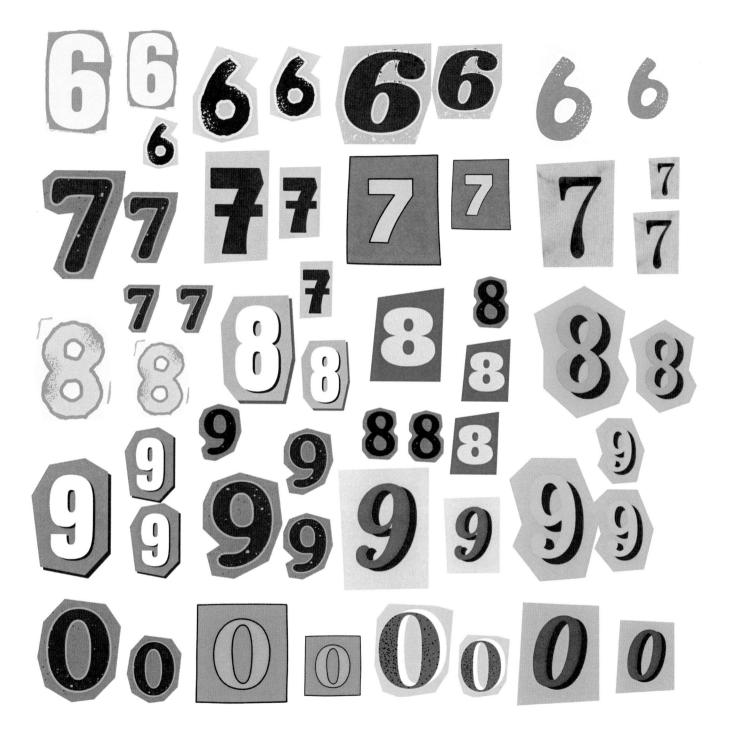

R r R r r r S S S
R r R r R r s s S S s s
R r T t T T T t T t
t L l L l T T n N N N
L l L l N n N N
L l L O N N n n N n N N

Made in the USA
Las Vegas, NV
11 December 2024

13737906R00043